spot the difference

USBORNE

Usborne Wipe-Clean

Nature Activities

Kirsteen Robson

Illustrated by
Manuela Berti

puzzles

mazes

connect the dots

1 2 3 4 5 6 7 8 9 10

drawing

Follow the trails to see which bee will land on a flower.

Connect the numbered dots in order, to finish the snail.

Count the ants, then trace over the numbers.

Usborne Wipe-Clean

Nature Activities

Illustrated by Manuela Berti
Designed by Laura Hammonds
Written by Kirsteen Robson

Use your wipe-clean pen to do all the activities in this fun-filled book.

6 7 8 9 10

At the pond

Follow the trails to see which froglet will join its father on the lily pad.

Use the pen to finish drawing the black frogspawn.

Draw a line between each matching pair of dragonflies.

Spot 3 differences between the two herons above.

Country park

Use the pen to show the rabbits the way to their family.

Connect the numbered dots in order, to finish the tree.

Draw 3 more eggs in the nest above.

Find and circle 6 butterflies.

On the beach

Count the shells in each group, then trace over the numbers.

3 5 6

Draw over the dotted lines to finish these two starfish.

Follow the trails to see which little plover bird will reach the sea.

Write an X under the crab that does not match the others.

Tiny world

Draw around the leaf that has the most nibbles taken out of it.

Spot 3 differences between these two snails.

Connect the numbered dots in order, to finish the spider's web.

Find and circle 7 bees.

Draw over the dotted lines to finish the two butterflies.

On the cliffs

Follow the trails to see which gull will land on the cliff.

Write an X under the puffin below that does not match the others.

Draw over the dotted lines to finish the beams of light.

Count the razorbill birds in each group below, then trace over the numbers.

Find another bird like this one.

On the river

Spot 3 differences between these two kingfisher birds.

Connect the numbered dots in order, to finish this swan.

Count the ducklings below, then trace over the correct number.

Follow the trails to see which otter will reach the riverbank.

Find and circle 5 dragonflies.

Woodland walk

Use the pen to show the squirrel the way to his two squirrel friends.

Draw over the dotted lines to finish the leaves.

Write an X under the deer that does not match the others.

Find and circle 4 mice.

Mountain wildlife

Follow the trails to see which beaver will swim to the dam.

Draw a line between each matching pair of pikas below.

Count the bear cubs, then trace over the correct number below.

5 6 7

Draw over the dotted lines to finish the sheep's horns.

Northern forest

Use the pen to show the two caribou the way to the rest of their herd.

Spot 5 differences between these two crossbill birds.

Find and circle 4 snowshoe hares.

Draw over the dotted lines to finish the skunk's tail.

Nature at night

Follow the trails to see which bat will fly up to the branch.

Draw a line between each pair of matching moths.

Count all the stars in the picture, then trace over the correct number.

8 9 10

Draw over the dotted lines to finish the owl.

Usborne

Wipe-Clean

Nature Activities

This fun book is a perfect way for young children to develop their counting, observation and pen control skills.

US $8.99

CAN $11.99

JFM MJJASOND/25 7740/5

Ink from pen may not be washable.
L'encre du feutre ne s'efface pas toujours au lavage.
This product conforms to ASTM D 4236.

WARNING! Not suitable for children under 36 months because of small parts. Choking hazard.

ATTENTION! Ne convient pas aux enfants de moins de 36 mois en raison des petites pièces. Risque de suffocation par ingestion.

⚠ WARNING:
CHOKING HAZARD—Small parts.
Not for children under 3 yrs.

usborne.com

FSC www.fsc.org MIX Paper | Supporting responsible forestry FSC® C017606

ISBN 978-1-83605-112-1

50899

9 781836 051121

Usborne Publishing Limited, 83–85 Saffron Hill, London EC1N 8RT, United Kingdom. Printed in China.